Virtual Reality Developer

Other titles in the *Cutting Edge Careers* series include:

Virtual Reality Developer

Kathryn Hulick

ReferencePoint Press®

San Diego, CA

© 2018 ReferencePoint Press, Inc.
Printed in the United States

For more information, contact:
ReferencePoint Press, Inc.
PO Box 27779
San Diego, CA 92198
www.ReferencePointPress.com

LIBRARY OF CONGRESS CATALOGING-IN-PUBLICATION DATA

Name: Hulick, Kathryn, author.
Title: Virtual Reality Developer/by Kathryn Hulick.
Description: San Diego, CA: ReferencePoint Press, Inc., [2018] | Series: Cutting Edge Careers |
    Audience: Grade 9 to 12. | Includes bibliographical references and index.
Identifiers: LCCN 2017019780 (print) | LCCN 2017029963 (ebook) | ISBN 9781682821916 (eBook)
    | ISBN 9781682821909 (hardback)
Subjects: LCSH: Virtual reality—Vocational guidance. | Computer software—Development—
    Vocational guidance. | Computer software developers.
Classification: LCC QA76.25 (ebook) | LCC QA76.25 .H85 2018 (print) | DDC 006.8023—dc23
LC record available at https://lccn.loc.gov/2017019780

CONTENTS

VIRTUAL REALITY DEVELOPER AT A GLANCE

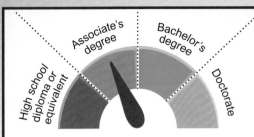

Minimum Educational Requirements

High school diploma or equivalent
Associate's degree
Bachelor's degree
Doctorate

Personal Qualities

- ☑ Creativity
- ☑ Adaptability
- ☑ Openness to taking risks
- ☑ Artistic
- ☑ Analytical skills

Working Conditions

Office

Pay   Averages $100,690* per year

Technical Skills

Gaming

3-D rendering

Programming language, especially C++

Predicted from 2014 to 2024*

17%

Future Job Outlook

*numbers are for software developers,
a group that includes virtual reality developers

Source: Bureau of Labor Statistics, *Occupational Outlook Handbook*. www.bls.gov.

A Whole New Reality

Imagine going on a field trip to the moon. You step out of the space shuttle and then bounce up, high above the lunar surface, feeling almost weightless in the low gravity. However, you are not really on the moon. You are standing in a room on Earth with a pair of virtual reality goggles covering your eyes.

Most people are used to interacting with the digital world through screens. We tap, swipe, and click to control devices. We view content and enjoy media on a flat, backlit surface that is clearly separate from the three-dimensional (3-D) world. Virtual reality (VR) and augmented reality promise to change all of this. Virtual reality puts the user inside the scene, replacing the real world with a digital realm that he or she can explore in three dimensions. Users can see, hear, or even touch virtual objects. Augmented reality (also called mixed reality) brings digital content to the real world as holograms or an overlay of text or images. Both forms of technology promise to upend the way people interact with work, entertainment, and each other.

Virtual reality is so different from any other form of technology that its creators have come up with their own term for virtual games, movies, and other content. They call them *experiences*. In virtual reality, you do not just watch or listen or play—you experience a whole new world.

Experiencing Other Realities

Many people were introduced to augmented reality during the summer of 2016, when the popular game Pokémon Go was released. Suddenly, all over the United States, people could be seen walking around their towns or cities, cell phones close to their faces, scanning their real environments for elusive Pokémon characters. The game uses a cell phone's camera to view the real world and then adds digital monsters into the scene. Players travel to real locations—their local coffee shop or playground—to capture these creatures. Another kind of augmented reality features glasses that display digital content in the wearer's field of vision but still allow the person to see the environment around them. Google Glass was the first example of such a commercial product. Although that product has since been discontinued, Epson currently produces a pair of smart glasses called Moverio that also overlays text onto the real world. A different product by Microsoft—the HoloLens—takes augmented reality to another level, projecting holograms out into the real world.

Standard cell phones now offer immersive virtual reality experiences with the help of viewers such as Google Cardboard. The viewer— which really is made of cardboard—features two simple lenses that allow the user to view virtual reality content, including 360-degree video, on the phone's screen. The user simply inserts his or her phone into the viewer and then wears it as a headset. Google Daydream and Samsung Gear VR offer a similar, though better-quality, virtual reality experience on a smartphone. Higher-end virtual reality headsets such as the Oculus Rift, HTC Vive, and Sony PlayStation VR—all of which came out in 2015 or 2016— provide an even more realistic experience. Some virtual reality systems include add-on components such as motion-tracking gloves and vests and handheld controllers that allow the user to physically move through a scene, take actions, and perhaps even "touch" virtual objects.

A Brand New Industry

As of late 2017, many of these virtual and augmented reality devices remained outside of mainstream culture. Typically, only avid gamers or people who work in technology or media have had the chance to experience cutting-edge virtual reality. Companies are reluctant to create games or apps for virtual reality unless they know that people are going to buy and use the devices. However, people will not buy expensive headsets and other equipment unless they have awesome games to play or important apps to use.

virtual reality products. A game engine streamlines the development process, making it possible to adjust the work in progress using visual interfaces such as buttons and sliders. Developers who want features that are not available in the basic game engine can often find a plug-in that has those features available.

In addition to game engines, VR developers have access to a plethora of information online, including open-source virtual reality software. These are programs that have been posted in their entirety for anyone to download and modify. Zeighami explains that when he needs to add something to a program or fix a problem, he searches for a solution on Google. "Ninety-nine percent of the time, someone else has a code snippet. I copy their code and make modifications." If he cannot find an answer, he can post his question in a forum and get an answer from others who have solved similar issues. "It's a very fast workflow. Between Googling and modifying code, I can knock out a problem in less than five minutes."[6]

After developers and programmers create new software, they have to test it to see if it works as expected. Some tests look for errors called bugs, which may disrupt the program or cause unwanted behavior. Others look for performance issues that may make the program run slowly or crash. Some testing may be done manually, but many tests are conducted by additional computer programs that developers, programmers, or testing personnel write. Developers and programmers work together to address issues that arise during testing.

The user's experience while interacting with the program also matters; thus, a lot of testing goes toward making this the best experience possible. User-experience testing is by nature much more subjective than other types of testing because everyone experiences reality—even virtual reality—differently. For example, some immersive programs and games make users feel as though they are moving, running, or falling. These sensations may not bother some users but may cause extreme motion sickness in others. Erickson says that the first rule of virtual reality design is "do not make the user sick!"[7]

Once a virtual reality program is out in the world, VR developers

Companies at the Cutting Edge of VR

The major players in the burgeoning alternate-reality industry are the companies that produce VR devices. Facebook owns the company Oculus, which makes the Oculus Rift headset. Microsoft has an augmented reality product called the HoloLens. Sony, the maker of PlayStation, produces the PlayStation VR, and the video game company Valve partnered with the consumer electronics company HTC to create the Vive, which is a VR device for gaming. Samsung produces a VR viewing device called the Samsung Gear VR, and Google makes the Cardboard and the Daydream.

All of these companies had already established themselves in the tech industry before they began developing virtual reality devices. However, they are not the only ones bringing virtual reality into the world. "Microsoft and Oculus/Facebook—the two largest employers—account for less than 2% of all VR gaming professionals," says Jeremy Schifeling, chief executive officer (CEO) of Break Into Tech. The majority of virtual reality developers work for small companies and start-ups.

Quoted in Caroline Zaayer Kaufman, "How to Land a Job in Virtual Reality Tech," Monster. www.monster.com.

are typically responsible for maintaining it. They may have to fix bugs or other issues that were not caught during testing. They may also develop and release add-ons or updates. At a smaller company, they may travel to conferences, expos, and other events to promote the product.

Games, Movies, and Beyond

When many people think of virtual reality, they picture immersive games and movies. This is in part because the video game industry was one of the first to experiment with this new form of media. In fact, Nintendo released a virtual reality gaming device called the Virtual Boy back in 1995. The technology was too far ahead of its time, however, and flopped.

Today the technology has improved to the point that consumers are much more likely to embrace it, and video gaming has kicked off a revival of the virtual reality industry. Most of the high-end headsets currently available were produced either by video game companies or with gamers in mind as a target audience. Zeighami has made these kinds of games for virtual reality. His company produces a racquetball-like virtual reality game called Smackitball, and he is currently working on a motorcycle action game called Redline that he hopes will make it into arcades. Entertainment, media, and marketing companies have also turned to virtual reality to produce immersive movies, news, documentaries, and advertisements. Many virtual reality developers will find opportunities to work in these areas. However, jobs in many other industries are also available.

Shauna Heller, who worked for Oculus before founding her own company, Clay Park VR, explains that the Oculus was mainly intended for games and entertainment when it was launched. But her job was to support developers who were creating many other kinds of virtual reality content. "Anyone who fell outside of a traditional game or a traditional piece of entertainment came to me," she says. "That included arts, culture, architecture, enterprise, medicine, health, science, space, theme parks, visual effects, and education."[8] In her opinion, virtual reality has incredible potential as a tool to make a difference in just about any industry. Zeighami agrees. "I don't see VR games as what's going to be the biggest category of VR usage out there," he says. As an example of something that is moving faster than games, he points to architectural visualization software. These are programs that allow architects to design buildings in three dimensions. Compared to flat programs that attempt to

"Industries like architecture, engineering, and construction will undoubtedly use VR for 3D design, [while] medical, military and education [industries] will certainly take advantage of the tech to do simulations, safety training, or to enable people to experience and explore remote places or uninhabitable environments."[10]

—Nate Beatty, cofounder of IrisVR

model a 3-D building, "virtual reality is just such a better solution,"[9] says Zeighami. One reason is because this software lets architects walk around inside a model of a building as they design it.

Virtual reality developers could find themselves working on similar modeling programs for a variety of products, from cars to bridges. "Industries like architecture, engineering, and construction will undoubtedly use VR for 3D design," says Nate Beatty, whose company specializes in virtual reality for architects. The potential for virtual reality to play a role in training and education is also huge. Says Beatty, "Medical, military and education [industries] will certainly take advantage of the tech to do simulations, safety training, or to enable people to experience and explore remote places or uninhabitable environments."[10] Finally, the virtual reality industry could create totally new markets. Virtual tourism could allow people to visit distant places and times, such as the bottom of the ocean or Egypt during the time of the pharaohs.

> "If you see a problem virtual reality could solve, you could be the one to solve it."[11]
>
> —Nima Zeighami, cofounder of VR Sports and a freelance developer

Because this technology is so new and has so much potential, many of its applications have yet to be imagined, let alone designed or developed. Zeighami says, "If you see a problem virtual reality could solve, you could be the one to solve it."[11]

CHAPTER 2

How Do You Become a Virtual Reality Developer?

Virtual reality is a brand new industry. Almost all of the developers currently working in virtual reality started out in a different field. Most were originally software engineers, programmers, or developers of web content, apps, or video games. Some began their career doing graphic art, 3-D animation, theater, journalism, or even filmmaking. The one thing all virtual reality developers have in common is that they taught themselves this new technology. They experimented with making virtual or augmented reality apps, tools, or games on their own time before getting hired to do so.

Though colleges and universities will likely start to offer more classes in virtual reality development, it is quite rare for formal school environments to offer such courses of study. The most reliable path to becoming a virtual reality developer is to sit down and develop an app, game, or tool in virtual reality. Of course, to do that a developer needs to have at least some basic technical skills in programming and application development. Formal degree programs can help students gain the background they need to jump into virtual reality. In addition, a multitude of resources, many of them freely available online, are available to walk a beginner through the process of making his or her first virtual reality app.

From Computer Science and Video Games to 3-D Art

A bachelor's or associate's degree in software engineering or computer science is the best first step to take toward achieving a career as a virtual reality developer. These degree programs

Virtual reality and video game development have a lot in common, including similar software tools and engines. This explains why gaming and game development experience is good preparation for virtual reality developers.

provide students with a solid technical foundation, including mastery of at least one programming language, an essential skill in any software development role. Of the many programming languages out there, C++, C#, and JavaScript are all great places to start. "I always recommend C++," says Nima Zeighami. "C++ is the graphics and games industry standard."[12] However, Zeighami and others recommend not getting too hung up on which specific programming language to learn. "Real developers are going to touch dozens of languages in a lifetime," says Josh Farkas, CEO of the company Cubicle Ninjas, which crafts custom virtual reality experiences for businesses. He stresses that the real question is not which language to learn but rather how quickly one can learn new languages. "If you were asked next year to switch to a different language, could you do that?"[13]

Indeed, the virtual reality industry changes so rapidly that it is impossible to learn everything needed for a job while in school. New tools, technologies, and programming languages become available all the time and constantly shift in popularity and usage.

Rather than focusing on specific programming languages or tools, aspiring VR developers should use their time as a student to develop their ability to think, reason, and solve programming problems. Anyone who wants to become a VR developer should get used to experimenting with new software and hardware as they become available.

That said, there are some specific technical skills that are essential and foundational for a career in virtual reality development. Immersive virtual experiences take place in 3-D space. Therefore, virtual reality developers must be comfortable working with 3-D environments, characters, and graphics. They must understand the physics and geometry that govern interactions in this space. They must also master 3-D rendering, which is the process used to draw a 3-D scene or create 3-D animation. Neal Nellans, founder and CEO of Ghost Machine VR Studios, has the following advice for burgeoning VR developers: "Play around with getting objects to move in 3D space. From a developing standpoint, virtual reality development is not much different from standard real-time 3D development."[14] An Xbox or PlayStation video game is an example of a standard real-time 3-D application.

In fact, video game development in general has a lot in common with virtual reality development. The obvious connection is that one of the popular ways to experience virtual reality is by playing games, and many virtual reality developers do, in fact, make games. However, the connection goes deeper than that. Consider that in a movie that uses 3-D animation, the scenes are crafted ahead of time and are not subject to change. But in games, characters and objects in the 3-D environment must continually update their appearance or orientation as players interact with them. Sounds and other forms of feedback also happen in real time. Virtual reality has the same requirements. Visuals, audio, and even tactile feedback change dynamically as users move their head and hands through the virtual space. The software tools required to build the realistic 3-D environments, characters,

"Don't wait for tomorrow! Dive in, get your hands dirty, and have fun."[17]

—Josh Farkas, CEO of Cubicle Ninjas

Game Development Programs

A degree in game development is beneficial for students interested in working in virtual reality, especially if their goal is to build VR games. Game development programs have become quite popular at both community colleges and four-year colleges and universities. Common classes include applied linear algebra, software development in C++, scripting for games, 3-D modeling, interactive animation, and artificial intelligence.

However, completing such a program does not guarantee one will land a job working on games. Breaking into such a popular industry takes a combination of skill, networking, and luck. If you decide to pursue a game development degree, be sure to focus on developing technical skills in programming and application development in general. That way, you can get a regular software development job to earn money while using your free time to make games and try to break into the games side of the industry.

and graphics of many modern video games translate well to any immersive virtual experience, whether it is a game or not. In fact, the easiest way to create an application for virtual reality is to build it in a game engine, typically Unity 3D or Unreal Engine. These engines provide a suite of tools that make it possible to build a game or virtual reality application without extensive programming knowledge, and both are free for students to download and try.

If programming is not your passion, do not worry. Although VR developers need some programming experience, many do not have that as their main area of focus. Courses in 3-D art and animation can also help students embark on a career in the virtual reality industry. In these classes, students learn programs such as Blender, Maya, and 3ds Max, all of which provide tools that allow artists and developers to draw, animate, and render characters and objects in 3-D. In addition, game engines can do most of the heavy lifting of coding a virtual reality application. This means that rather than writing lines of code, users can move sliders or check off boxes to change their program.

A Friendly Face

You might think that creating a captivating and technically excellent virtual reality app would be enough to achieve success in the industry. However, that is not always the case. VR developers also need to be warm, conversational, and kind when they meet others in the industry—for example, at a conference or networking event. "You have to be friendly and open-minded," says Nima Zeighami, cofounder of VR Sports. "It's not always about raw talent."

Even though being friendly has nothing to do with programming or technology, friendliness does help VR developers make connections with others in the industry. These relationships are essential for brokering new business deals or finding new customers. Networking is especially important for those who work as freelancers or independent contractors. Zeighami says it took two years of working in virtual reality before people started to recognize him and treat him as one of the inner circle. The community can be extremely supportive and helpful, he says, but it may not accept a person who arrives on the scene acting like he or she already knows everything. Being open and friendly can go a long way toward building a critical network of fellow developers who can help grow a career.

Nima Zeighami, interview with the author, March 31, 2017.

product that does not even run on a new generation of devices.

Given this ever-changing environment, developers must adapt quickly to updates as they happen. Anyone who wants to work in virtual reality should be prepared to constantly keep an eye out for new products, software tools, standards of design, and more. Nima Zeighami spends up to an hour every day just reading about what is new in the VR industry. Farkas says that a virtual reality developer must be prepared to confront a new technology that he or she has never seen before in the morning and then present a working prototype made with the new technology that afternoon.

As such, people who enjoy teaching themselves novel technology and like to continually learn new things do very well in this

Virtual reality developers usually do not work alone. Most projects require teams of developers, artists, designers, filmmakers, and project managers to share ideas and work together to solve problems.

field. "The most important skill to have if you want to become a VR developer is to be willing to play around and break things,"[23] says Erickson. After you break something, of course, you have to figure out how to fix it. That process of analyzing the problem and addressing it develops new skills and knowledge.

Pioneers of New Technology

Although constant change can be frustrating, tiring, or even intimidating to developers, it can also be very exciting. Indeed, this is one job that never gets boring. "VR is uncharted territory," says Pablo Varias Navarro, founder of Zenva, an organization that offers online courses in game development and virtual reality. "We are all learning as we go, and this requires me to spend a lot of time reading, watching videos and testing what works and what doesn't with the different devices that I own."[24]

Because virtual reality is such a brand new field, developers have a lot of freedom in the way they build new virtual reality tools and experiences. "Virtual reality is a new medium and while there are some guidelines emerging, it's still very early and very much the wild west,"[25] says Lee Wasilenko, founder of VR Dev School.

The fact that there are not very many standards or industry best practices to follow sometimes has its downside, however. For example, it is almost impossible to ensure that a new game, app, or software tool will be compatible with all virtual reality hardware. "Not all devices have the same features," explains Navarro. "For instance, if you jump in real life in the HTC Vive, you also jump in the virtual world, but this doesn't happen with the Gear VR or the Cardboard."[26] People who are bothered by this kind of inconsistency, or those who thrive in situations with a lot of structure and well-defined rules, might not be right for this career. However, those who enjoy having freedom to experiment and explore would be well suited to working in virtual reality.

> "The most important skill to have if you want to become a VR developer is to be willing to play around and break things."[23]
>
> —Liv Erickson, a virtual reality developer at High Fidelity

Sometimes these experiments pay off. For example, Zeighami came up with the term *room sync*, which is now used by others in the industry to refer to any process that syncs the positions of players in a virtual room to their positions in a real room. Syncing helps them avoid bumping into each other while immersed in a virtual experience. "Being a pioneer is an interesting process," says Zeighami. "You create what the industry is and does."[27]

Indeed, virtual reality developers are currently defining the way people perform simple acts like making purchases, accessing menus, linking to friends, and more. VR developers have to think outside the box to imagine how users could undertake these actions in virtual reality. Conventional solutions, such as clickable menus, may work on a flat screen but could be cumbersome in an immersive environment. "How do you take a tour in VR? What level of control can you give a user? What story potential is there? We still don't really know,"[28] says Farkas. Navarro adds that no one has any preconceptions or assumptions about how things should work: "In this new arena everyone has a fair chance to make something big."[29]

CHAPTER 4

What Is It like to Work as a Virtual Reality Developer?

Working in virtual reality is exciting, collaborative, and full of surprises. Josh Farkas describes the role as "a merge between application or web development and an entertainment job like a TV show."[30] There is plenty of technical work to be done, but there is also a lot of storytelling and art involved.

The day-to-day reality of working as a VR developer depends a lot on where the work takes place. Some virtual reality developers work at well-established companies such as Google or Microsoft. However, many more work at small start-up companies or as freelance developers who bounce from contract to contract. Silicon Valley, the capital of the tech world, is home to many virtual reality and augmented reality start-ups, so many VR developers live nearby in Northern California. Whether a developer is part of a large company or a small start-up, or works independently, the job is full of freedom and variety. The virtual reality department is typically one of a company's more experimental areas. No one really knows yet which virtual reality products will be most successful or even the best way to create them. As a result, developers often get a lot of say in defining their own roles.

The Daily Routine

A VR developer's daily routine depends on the size of the company where he or she works and on the project in development. At a large company, a developer may focus on developing just one aspect of a project, such as the user interface for a new piece of software. At a start-up, a developer usually gets involved in many aspects of the project, even nontechnical roles involving art,

Two members of a development team test a new virtual reality product. Women and minorities are underrepresented in the industry, but tech companies are making efforts to improve diversity in their workforces.

design, marketing, or customer service. A freelance VR developer does everything, though he or she may reach out to other contractors for help completing portions of a complex project.

In a project's early phase, developers create prototypes or mock-ups of the application they plan to develop. They consider the aesthetics of the product and think about how users will interact with it. Then the team gets to work. As they build the application, they also spend a lot of time talking about it and testing it. Each new feature brings up new questions that may not have been considered during the design phase. "A lot of software development is iterative [repetitive] testing and trying," says Farkas. "We'll sit down ten times a day and test different software."[31]

When possible, developers rely on user testing as well. Developers may be too deep into the project to notice things that might be difficult or frustrating for users. Seeing which problems users encounter as they engage with a product highlights which areas need to be fixed. Francesca Panetta, who leads a VR team at the *Guardian*, a British newspaper, learned this firsthand. In 2016 her team was working on a new project that would allow users to explore the sewers under London. When they opened it up to user testing, they got interesting results. "People who've tested the experience are getting lost in the maze of subterranean sewers,"[32] she said. Her team therefore considered blocking off paths.

Tough Deadlines

When a project's deadline approaches, developers often experience a lot of stress and extra pressure at work. Christina Heller remembers how this was the case when her team was up against a tight deadline for a VR experience on which they were working. "The team was feeling confident," she says. "Then the night before delivery, we had a huge windstorm and it knocked the power out. Suddenly all our computers were down. Our team figured out how to get a generator, plugged in only the necessary machines, and worked in the dark to deliver the piece on deadline."[33]

Even under ordinary circumstances, virtual reality developers often must go the extra mile to get the job done. "It's not uncommon to be here until eight or nine at night or working on the weekend," says Farkas. "Not because anybody asked us to, but because we want to solve that issue."[34] In the video game industry, long, grueling weeks of hard work are so common toward the end of a project that game developers have their own name for it: crunch time. When Broken Window Studios was developing a virtual reality game called Grave VR, "we crunched for around 3 weeks to release, with a 6-day delay,"[35] says Aby Moore, cofounder of the company.

> "It's a personal, down-to-earth, very chill environment."[36]
>
> —Josh Farkas, CEO of Cubicle Ninjas

A Casual, Collaborative Atmosphere

When it is not crunch time, the work atmosphere at a virtual reality start-up tends to be friendly and casual. "It's a personal, down-to-earth, very chill environment,"[36] says Farkas of his company, Cubicle Ninjas. His team has a lot of flexibility to work from home if they need to. Conversely, if they are all in the office, they often order in food to eat. Employees tend to wear comfortable clothing and enjoy hanging out together. Heller reports a similar atmosphere at her company, VR Playhouse. "We're all friends and not just coworkers," she says. "We've had to learn how to communicate about challenging issues in direct, honest ways."[37]

> "We're all friends and not just coworkers. We've had to learn how to communicate about challenging issues in direct, honest ways."[37]
>
> —Christina Heller, cofounder of VR Playhouse

To help encourage this sense of connection and community among coworkers, some companies opt for an open layout. For example, teams at Liv Erickson's company have open work spaces called pods. This helps them have easy access to each other when they need to join forces, which is often. "We all collaborate together on projects,"[38] she says. Her team is also very open with their software solutions. Their product is open-source software, which means that the code they write is freely available to all developers. The effect is kind of like an inventor sharing his or her blueprints for anyone to use, change, and improve upon. This kind of collaboration across companies is common throughout the virtual reality industry. Even independent contractors need to collaborate and communicate with others. For example, Nima Zeighami is a freelance virtual reality developer who works from a home office, but he too must work closely with his clients on a daily basis.

Women and Minorities in Virtual Reality

Although the tech industry has generally been criticized for being unwelcoming to women and developers from diverse backgrounds, virtual reality offers the chance for a fresh start. The problem is serious: The percentage of women graduating with computer science degrees dropped from 37 percent to just 18 percent between 1984 and 2014. As of 2016, diversity reports from Google, Microsoft, Facebook, and Twitter stated that their employee populations were on average 56 percent white, 37 percent Asian, 3 percent Hispanic, and 1 percent black.

A Day in the Life of a Virtual Reality Developer

Nima Zeighami is a freelance virtual reality developer. Here is how he spends a typical day on the job:

I usually wake up at around 9 or 10. I sleep in a little more than most people do. I go to the gym, come back, shower, and then after that I get to work. I just moved into a home office. First, I will go through all the VR news for the day. I go through that for 30 minutes to an hour, looking at any new technologies or new techniques that came out. Then after that, I open up Unreal Engine or Unity 3D and start working on virtual reality software. I will do that for five to eight hours while simultaneously using an app called Franz. It allows me to aggregate all of my different messaging services, including Slack channels. A lot of the world's developers are on these Slack channels. We communicate and share information there. If I ever have questions, I can drop a line there, or I can answer other people's questions. As I work on stuff, I'm also responding to e-mails and creating new contracts.

Nima Zeighami, interview with the author, March 30, 2017.

Over the past several years, major tech companies—including Facebook and Google—have made it a top priority to improve diversity. The virtual reality industry was born in the middle of this push to develop more diverse workforces. A mind-set that diversity is good for business has been present from the very beginning. "I haven't experienced discrimination," says Heller, a woman who is working in a traditionally male-dominated industry. "I've received encouragement from my peers."[39]

However, there is still work to do to attract more women and minorities to the industry. To try to bring attention to the issue,

Heller regularly speaks out about diversity at conferences and other events. At the 2016 Game Developers Conference, she hosted a panel of women who all run companies in the virtual reality industry. One of the panelists, Christine Cattano of Framestore VR Studio, said, "There are a lot of women on the production side. What I don't see a lot of diversity in is women as artists or engineers or programmers. I see maybe one for every fifty men."[40] Erickson is one of those female programmers. She has seen more awareness of diversity in the virtual reality industry than she did in previous roles in other parts of the tech industry. She hopes that one day the industry will not have to consider diversity because it will have become an accepted and normal part of business.

The Money Comes and Goes

One important reason for women and minorities to consider careers in virtual reality development is the potential to earn a high salary. Indeed, software development skills are highly marketable. Developers in the United States earn a median salary of $100,690. That is more than twice the amount most Americans make in one year. However, the average software developer works in a stable, established sector of the tech industry. Most virtual reality companies or virtual reality departments have only been around for a few years, and the salaries that VR developers earn vary wildly. In start-up companies, for example, salaries and bonuses may increase as the company receives funding. For example, the start-up company Magic Leap, which is working on a headset that will allow users to experience holograms that interact with the real world, managed to raise more than $1 billion from investors. This enormous influx of money allowed the company to attract experienced engineers and developers to its team by offering them six-figure salaries. As funding runs out, however, some developers may lose their jobs.

Freelance developers are paid on the basis of the number and quality of contracts they are able to secure. "There's not a ton of money in the industry yet," says Zeighami. "I'm able to make do—I get enough contracts. But I really wish there was more money in the games and software side of things. If you just have a game idea, it's impossible to keep a company afloat."[41] VR game developer Joe Radak learned this firsthand. He has lost more than $36,000 on a puzzle game he made for the HTC Vive. In general, developers in the gaming and entertainment industries will likely earn less than those working on virtual reality applications for businesses.

CHAPTER 5

Advancement and Other Job Opportunities

Virtual reality is a volatile, burgeoning field. As a result, career opportunities are driven by more than just work experience and technical skills. Opportunity, market trends, and the amount of risk people are willing to take also come into play, making for a very unpredictable but exciting career path. A virtual reality developer who starts his or her own company may catapult to CEO right out of college. If that start-up dies, the former CEO might end up at the bottom again, in a regular developer role.

Much of this upheaval is due to the fact that the virtual reality industry has only really been around since 2014. It is therefore hard to know what a career in this industry might look like in another ten or even twenty years. As Liv Erickson says, "I think some of the jobs that people may move upwards into in the VR industry may not even exist yet."[42]

Jumping Off the Ladder

VR departments at large, stable companies can offer their employees a career ladder that mirrors that of a typical software developer. Out of college, a qualified candidate typically gets a job as an entry-level developer. In this role, he or she is akin to an apprentice, working closely with more senior developers and engineers on their projects to learn how things are done. After approximately three to five years of experience, developers begin to take on their own projects.

At this point they will also start to lean toward either the management career track or the engineering career track. Erickson says, "Being able to lead content or engineering teams is one area that is definitely a place to grow."[43] As a manager, the developer will direct a team of other developers, engineers, designers, and artists. As an engineer, the developer will become an expert in the company's product and will take the lead on high-profile development projects.

Taking a position at a start-up company is akin to jumping off the career ladder and onto a trampoline. The pay is often lower than at large companies, but developers often have the opportunity to get paid in stock, making them partial owners of the company. If the company is successful or purchased by another company, that stock can pay out at much higher values than a salary. Promotions also abound at small companies and start-ups. There are opportunities to leap upward very quickly, and people can often achieve incredible success in a short period of time. "Your success as an individual becomes tied to how successful the company is," says Raylene Young, an engineer at Stripe, a start-up tech company. "If you're at a really great start up, that growth curve . . . is extremely steep."[44]

Since virtual reality is a new industry, there is even more room

Entry-level developers often work with lots of guidance from more senior staff. Once they learn what the company is looking for and how it wants to get there, new developers often get their own projects to work on.

for upward growth for young people just starting out. "You can very quickly become an expert in this space," says Josh Farkas. "Someone who comes in at this point and learns and grows can be ready in a year or two to start their own software company." Farkas leads his start-up company, Cubicle Ninjas, a group of thirty people, eight of whom are focused on virtual reality. "I'm almost like the coach of a team," he says. "As the product grows, the biggest thing I'm doing is motivating the team and getting them excited about how to solve really complex problems."[45]

> "Someone who comes in at this point and learns and grows can be ready in a year or two to start their own software company."[45]
>
> —Josh Farkas, CEO of Cubicle Ninjas

Virtual reality developers who have started their own companies have put themselves in the role of CEO at a young age. This can be quite challenging, especially for someone who lacks a lot of work experience. In fact, in 2016 investors in a start-up called Skully, which was working on an augmented reality motorcycle helmet, kicked the cofounders out of the company. The young cofounders had failed to meet customers' orders and caused a deal with a Chinese firm that wanted to acquire the company to fall through.

If a start-up does not do well—if it fails to get funding, if its product flops, or if it is unable to solve critical technical problems with its product—VR developers may come crashing back down to the bottom. They may become experts in a technology that goes nowhere, or they may work long, grueling hours for very little pay, only to end up with a product that nobody wants or that does not work. However, even if a start-up fails, a developer from this environment has typically gained a more far-reaching set of skills and experiences compared to someone who played it safe in a structured role at a large company.

Changing Course

Some VR developers find it necessary to get involved with other aspects of a virtual reality project and may eventually be able to use this experience to transition to a completely different role

The Value of Networking

Liv Erickson was a recent college graduate when she decided to leave a more traditional software development role for one in the VR industry. She went on Meetup, a website that helps people with similar interests get together in person, and joined a group called Silicon Valley Virtual Reality. From there, she started getting to know others in the industry. She learned that the Samsung Developer Conference had an option for participants to focus on virtual reality. She realized that the material she learned at the conference and the people she met there could help her get started on a new career path, so she decided to take a big chance. She took three days off work, using up her vacation days to attend the event, even though she knew nothing about it. "I loved everything about that week, and the momentum fueled me," she says.

Conferences, Meetups, and professional organizations offer valuable opportunities to network with others in the industry. These relationships help developers share knowledge and may also lead to new career opportunities. Going to conferences is now a part of Erickson's job, as she is responsible for convincing other developers to use her company's product, which is a platform for creating social virtual reality experiences.

Liv Erickson, *Entering the Metaverse: Your Guide to Joining the Virtual Reality Industry*. Seattle: Amazon Digital Services, 2016. Kindle edition.

within the industry. Some of the roles available to a VR developer who is looking to change course include designing stories, game levels, or user experiences in a virtual or augmented reality experience. Some might pivot to become animators or 3-D artists who create digital visuals or videographers who shoot movie-like experiences. Some might go into sound engineering, crafting audio effects and soundtracks. Still others might become producers or project managers who ensure that a project runs smoothly from beginning to end.

Some virtual reality developers may also transition to the hardware side of virtual reality. With experience in electrical or computer engineering, a person may get involved in designing and developing new headsets, augmented reality glasses, and other devices. An engineer may be responsible for building prototypes of a new device, including testing and selecting materials, sourcing technical components, and wiring everything together. Engineers also thoroughly test these devices to ensure that they work properly.

Lateral movement is quite common between the virtual reality industry and many other industries, from technology to entertainment. As a result, many virtual reality developers follow twisting career paths that veer from one industry to another. Many virtual reality developers started out working on other forms of technology, such as video games, computer software, websites, applications for tablets or mobile phones, or consumer electronics. This makes for teams that are well-rounded and have a breadth of skills. Shauna Heller of Clay Park VR can attest to this. She says the composition of a typical virtual reality team includes people of all different professional backgrounds and experiences:

> What I'm seeing in terms of successful teams are those that are bringing together a couple of people from the mobile world, a couple of people from the software, engineering side—your coders and programmers—a couple of people from the video game world, and then people from the visual effects and 3D design industry.[46]

However, the virtual reality industry has also pulled in talent from areas that seem unrelated. People with experience creating advertisements, television programs, movies, news pieces, documentaries, or even theater productions have found a calling in virtual reality. Similar kinds of media, such as 360-degree movies and immersive journalism, are being developed for virtual reality. "Our team comes from diverse backgrounds," says Christina Heller of VR Playhouse. "We've got theater, film, and animation. I'm a journalist by my background. We've got gamers."[47] Any experience telling stories and reaching an audience can be applied to work in virtual reality. Stepping into the virtual reality industry could be a career advancement option for someone from almost any background.

that it prompts people to go out and buy the new technology. For example, many consider text messaging to be a killer app that helped spread cell phone technology far and wide. Although many virtual reality applications are fun, inspiring, or even breathtaking, none have sparked widespread adoption of the technology thus far. The firm Strategy Analytics predicts that by the end of 2017, just 16 percent of adults in the United States will own a virtual reality headset, rising to around 27 percent by 2018.

However, many experts feel that the killer app will come along any day now. Helen Situ of NextVR says that the big draw of virtual reality is its ability to take you to places where you either want to teleport or time travel, such as to a sports event or concert. "Every fan wants to sit court side,"[54] she says. In the future, instead of watching the big game on television, fans could sit in the best seat in the stadium as the game is live-streamed in virtual reality. Or, even more exciting, users could experience the game as if they were one of the players. Similarly, they might feel the rush of standing onstage beside their favorite musical artist during a concert.

The ability to virtually teleport to be with friends and family near and far could also be what brings virtual reality into the mainstream. "The incredible thing about the technology is that you feel like you're actually present in another place with other people," says Mark Zuckerberg, CEO of Facebook. "People who try it say it's different from anything they've ever experienced in their lives." This is a main reason why Zuckerberg's company decided to acquire the VR firm Oculus. "This is really a new communication platform," says Zuckerberg. "By feeling truly present, you can share unbounded spaces and experiences with the people in your life. Imagine sharing not just moments with your friends online, but entire experiences and adventures."[55]

> "This is really a new communication platform. By feeling truly present, you can share unbounded spaces and experiences with the people in your life. Imagine sharing not just moments with your friends online, but entire experiences and adventures."[55]
>
> —Mark Zuckerberg, CEO of Facebook

In the future, rather than tagging friends in flat photos or videos, users could teleport together somewhere for a truly shared experience. They might one day also be able to record experiences, just as they currently take photos and videos. Then they could later transport themselves back into favorite memories that seem almost as real as the day they first experienced them. Just imagine—instead of watching a video of your last birthday party, you could be there again, tasting the cake and opening up your gifts.